I0443291

TABLE OF CONTENTS

4 TO COLOR

45 WORD SCRAMBLES

55 SUDOKUS

80 Sudokus answers

87 WORD SEARCH

96 WORD SEARCH ANSWERS

This book belongs to

to color

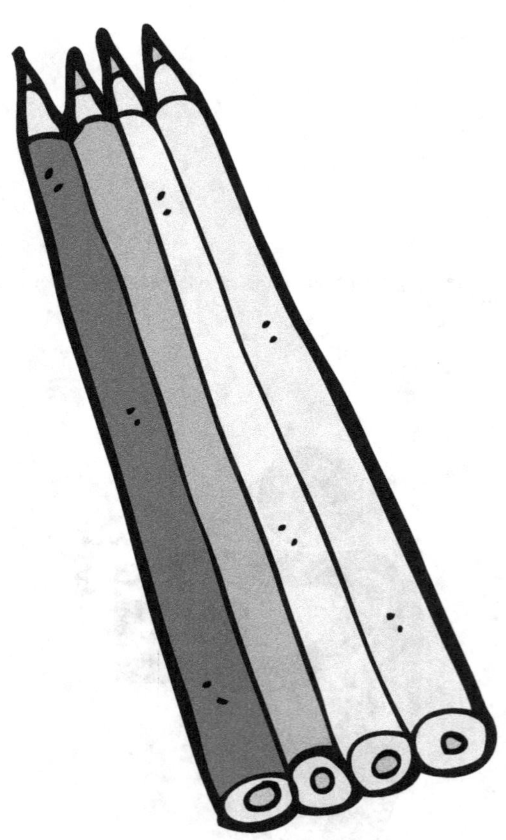

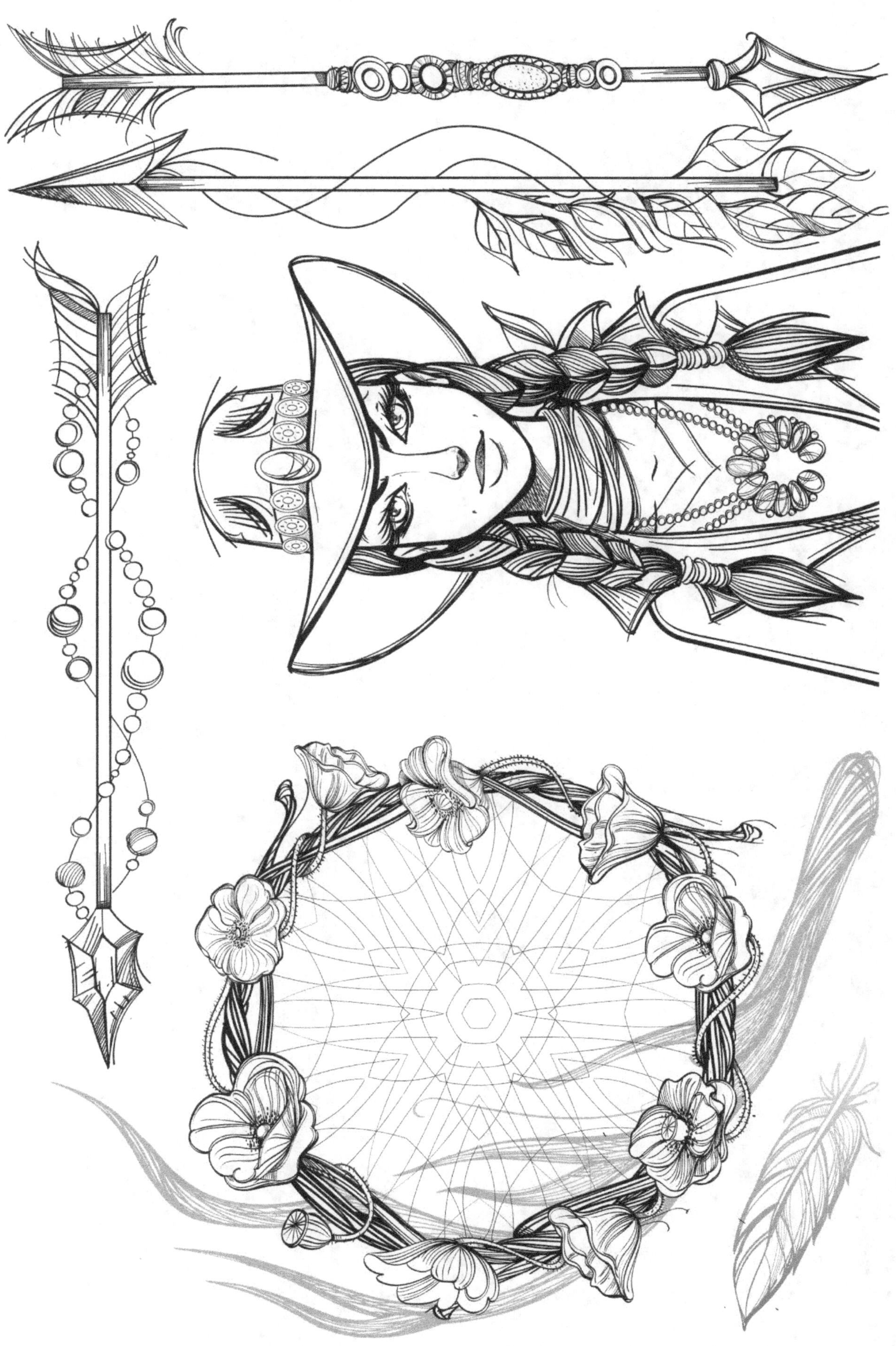

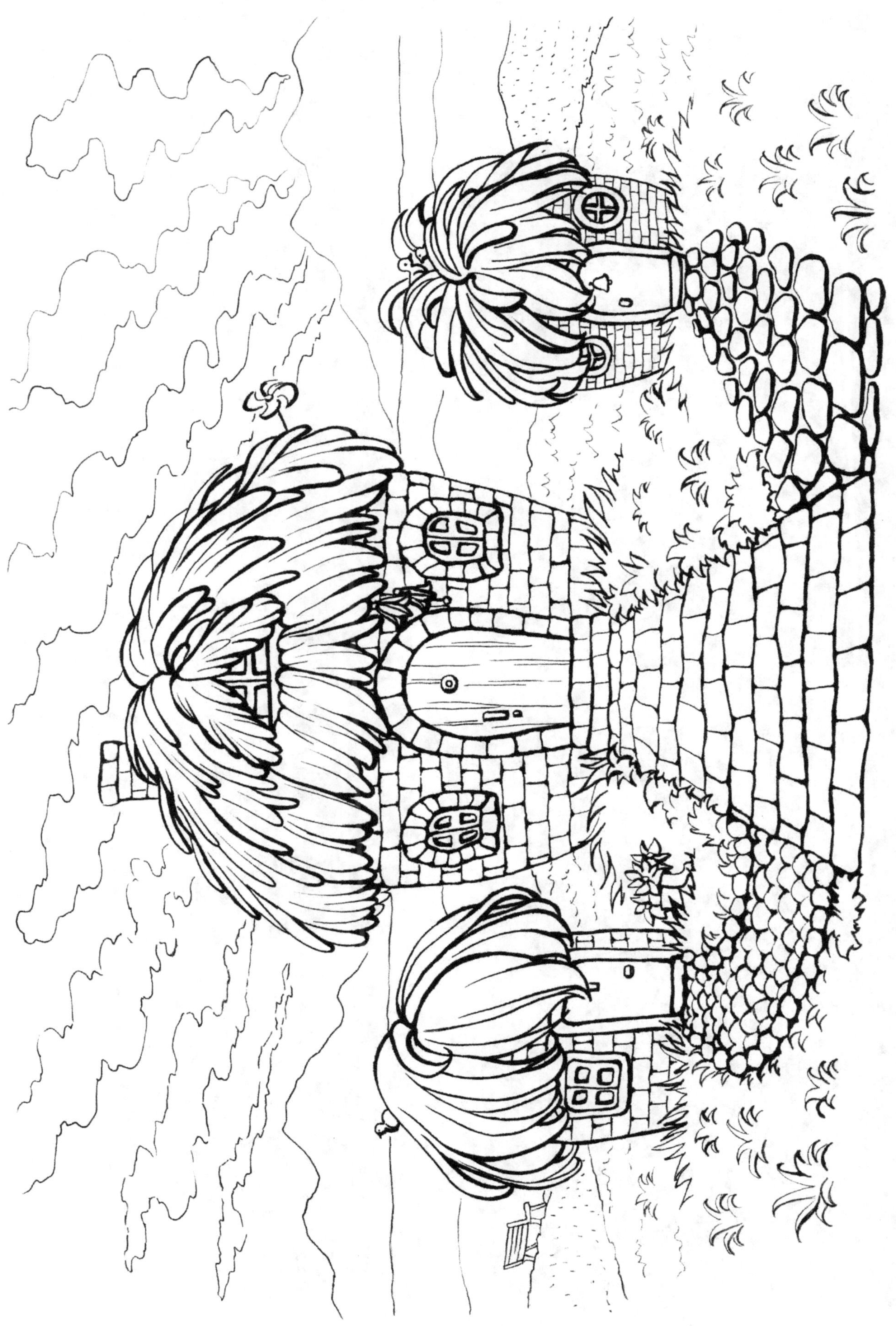

Word Scrambles

Puzzle #1

WINTER WEATHER

OBSOT	_ _ _ _ _
EPILRPC	_ _ _ _ _ _ _
EIC OGF	_ _ _ _ _ _ _
ARILZDBZ	_ _ _ _ _ _ _ _
EETSL	_ _ _ _ _
ONWS	_ _ _ _
RFSILREU	_ _ _ _ _ _ _ _
EIC	_ _ _
EREGFNZI	_ _ _ _ _ _ _ _
CIELCI	_ _ _ _ _ _
ETIR HSANCI	_ _ _ _ _ _ _ _ _ _ _
EHTUWTOI	_ _ _ _ _ _ _ _

Puzzle #2

DRUMS

ANCGSO _ _ _ _ _ _

ONOGBS _ _ _ _ _ _

AABTL _ _ _ _ _

RSHBUSE _ _ _ _ _ _ _

IMOTBARENU _ _ _ _ _ _ _ _ _ _

ISTSKC _ _ _ _ _ _

MTO MTO _ _ _ _ _ _ _

OWC LBEL _ _ _ _ _ _ _ _

ERANS _ _ _ _ _

TKSISC _ _ _ _ _ _

YACBLM _ _ _ _ _ _

GTLIRENA _ _ _ _ _ _ _ _

Puzzle #3

PHOTOGRAPHY

MCAARE	_ _ _ _ _ _
TIILGDA	_ _ _ _ _ _ _
IMFL	_ _ _ _
ASFLH	_ _ _ _ _
REELGNA	_ _ _ _ _ _ _
GILHT	_ _ _ _ _
UCFSO	_ _ _ _ _
POELEVD	_ _ _ _ _ _ _
TNPIR	_ _ _ _ _
TOTIRPAR	_ _ _ _ _ _ _ _
NASEAPLDC	_ _ _ _ _ _ _ _ _
UXRSPEEO	_ _ _ _ _ _ _ _

Puzzle #4

MUSIC CLASS

GLAEROL _ _ _ _ _ _ _

PROGAIEG _ _ _ _ _ _ _ _

ATBE _ _ _ _

HCORD _ _ _ _ _

LCFE _ _ _ _

LTFA _ _ _ _

MHRYNOA _ _ _ _ _ _ _

ZAJZ _ _ _ _

EYK _ _ _

ROMAJ _ _ _ _ _

RUASMEE _ _ _ _ _ _ _

LOMEYD _ _ _ _ _ _

answers

Word Scrambles

Puzzle #1

WINTER WEATHER

OBSOT	=	BOOTS
EPILRPC	=	CLIPPER
EIC OGF	=	ICE FOG
ARILZDBZ	=	BLIZZARD
EETSL	=	SLEET
ONWS	=	SNOW
RFSILREU	=	FLURRIES
EIC	=	ICE
EREGFNZI	=	FREEZING
CIELCI	=	ICICLE
ETIR HSANCI	=	TIRE CHAINS
EHTUWTOI	=	WHITEOUT

Puzzle #2

DRUMS

ANCGSO	=	CONGAS
ONOGBS	=	BONGOS
AABTL	=	TABLA
RSHBUSE	=	BRUSHES
IMOTBARENU	=	TAMBOURINE
ISTSKC	=	STICKS
MTO MTO	=	TOM TOM
OWC LBEL	=	COW BELL
ERANS	=	SNARE
TKSISC	=	STICKS
YACBLM	=	CYMBAL
GTLIRENA	=	TRIANGLE

Puzzle #3

PHOTOGRAPHY

MCAARE	=	CAMERA
TIILGDA	=	DIGITAL
IMFL	=	FILM
ASFLH	=	FLASH
REELGNA	=	ENLARGE
GILHT	=	LIGHT
UCFSO	=	FOCUS
POELEVD	=	DEVELOP
TNPIR	=	PRINT
TOTIRPAR	=	PORTRAIT
NASEAPLDC	=	LANDSCAPE
UXRSPEEO	=	EXPOSURE

Puzzle #4

MUSIC CLASS

GLAEROL	=	ALLEGRO
PROGAIEG	=	ARPEGGIO
ATBE	=	BEAT
HCORD	=	CHORD
LCFE	=	CLEF
LTFA	=	FLAT
MHRYNOA	=	HARMONY
ZAJZ	=	JAZZ
EYK	=	KEY
ROMAJ	=	MAJOR
RUASMEE	=	MEASURE
LOMEYD	=	MELODY

Sudokus

Puzzle #1

MEDIUM

8		1						
		3			6			
			8		2		5	
1	3				9	6	7	
	6	8	7					4
	9		2	6	3			
7		4					1	6
9					1		2	5
	1			5		7		

Puzzle #2

MEDIUM

		7						
6		5	7					
4			2	3			9	5
	2	9		7			1	4
	5			4	1		6	
					2			8
						4	5	
		1	5	8	9			7
		2				9	8	3

Puzzle #3

MEDIUM

		6			4			8
1			3					
			9		7		6	1
	2	4	7					3
7				9	6	1		
	8			3		7	5	
3				2		8		7
2			6	7				
8						2		6

Puzzle #4

MEDIUM

		2		4	5			
6		8				9		3
	1		9			2		
		9			4			7
		1	8	7		6		
2				5				1
	9							2
	2	3			7	8		4
4				6			3	9

Puzzle #5

MEDIUM

8				4	6	3	7	1
	4	7			9		8	
		3	5					2
3		1	4	7		8		
	6	4					1	
		8	6	9				
	9							
7		6	8					
1				5				4

Puzzle #6

MEDIUM

	1			5	6	9	3	7
			2		9	8		
		6					5	2
8				1		2		
4		2	8		3		7	
	7						8	
3				2		7		5
			9	3		1		8
1	4		5					

Puzzle #7

MEDIUM

7	6	3		4		9		
1					2			
	5	2	6					3
6				9		3	1	
	4		2		6		7	
	1	5				6	4	
	7	6						
					8			
	9		5		7	2		4

Puzzle #8

MEDIUM

8	2				3		7	4
	9				1	3	5	2
6	5							
2	8		7	1	5	9		3
	7		9		4		8	5
		8		5				
							1	7
	1		6			8		

Puzzle #9

MEDIUM

9	5				2	4	6	1
					1		9	8
2								
	4	5		1			3	7
				8			4	
		8	6	3			2	
		2				6		
4	1	7	9	6	3			
	9				7			4

Puzzle #10

MEDIUM

		3				5		2
	2	1	4		6			
		6	8			1		4
	4	5	2	9		7	8	
		7		4		6		9
			7		5			
	5	8	9			3		
		2		3		9		
3	9						1	

Puzzle #11

MEDIUM

	2	8				3		
3		9			2		7	5
5	1		4					
	6					5	8	
		1		8	4			
8				6	9	2		4
7	9	3						8
			7					6
	5	6	8			7	9	

Puzzle #12

MEDIUM

		2					3	1
	1	8				7	9	
								5
8				7		6	5	
		6	5	2	8			
7	4		9			1		
6	8	1		3				7
4		9			7			8
	5			1	4			

Puzzle #13

MEDIUM

		9				3		8
6		3		5		7	4	
	2	1		8				5
3	6		9			8	2	
						9		
1		8	3	7	2		5	
	5	6						
		2		6	7		8	
					4			9

Puzzle #14

MEDIUM

				9	8		3	2
9	6	2	5		3			
4			6		1	7	5	
1			9	6				
5		4						1
					2		8	
	5							6
8				1				7
3			8	4	6	1		5

Puzzle #15

MEDIUM

	3			9				
9	2		7		1			4
	8			6				
3		6	8			1		9
8	9		5	1			6	
	5						4	
	7				6		8	5
5					3		9	6
4			9		8		7	

Puzzle #16

MEDIUM

	5				2	8		
4	9			7			6	5
3			6		1	4		
1					8	2		
					5	9	4	
5		9		4	7			
	3						1	
	2	5	1		6	7		
		4		2				6

Puzzle #17

MEDIUM

		1				7	3	
		2	4	5		8		
	9		7			1		
	1			8	4			
4	6	9	5			2	8	
	5			7	6			
	7		3					
9		6		2				4
5				4				6

Puzzle #18

MEDIUM

5							9	7
	1			5		6		
3	9		6		8			
					7		5	1
		8	3		6	4		
9	4	7			1			2
		1			9			
8	7	5	2			9		
			8				3	6

Puzzle #19

MEDIUM

7					9	6		
	2	4		8		9		5
1					6			3
5			9				2	8
	4	8				5		
		6		3	8			
8	9	1		7			4	
		2						1
3	7		4			8		

Puzzle #20

MEDIUM

	6	4		7	9		3	5
2				8		1		
		5						
		1					8	
	7			6	2		9	
				4	7	3	5	2
8		2		1	6		4	
			3		5			
	1							7

Puzzle #21

MEDIUM

	8	9	7	2	4			
				8		9	6	
5		4			9			7
						6		
		1	4	3			9	
7					1	4		
		3	6	4		8	7	
			8	1		5		
2				9			3	6

Puzzle #22

MEDIUM

							7	2
7				1	2	8		
	8	2	5		9			
	5				3	4		8
	1	9	7	6	8			
6				4				1
1								7
		4	3				1	9
	7		6	5				4

Puzzle #23

MEDIUM

	9		3		4		1	
7	2					5		
3			2	9				8
2		5		4	3			7
		3	7	6			5	
1				8				
			4			6		
	5		6	3	7			1
	4			2		7	3	

Puzzle #24

MEDIUM

			9		8		6	5
8	6	5				7		4
		1	6	7		3		
	1		8	9			7	3
	8	4			3		1	
6	4		3				5	1
5	7	8	1				3	
		9						

Sudokus

answers

Puzzle # 1

8	4	1	5	3	7	2	6	9
5	2	3	1	9	6	8	4	7
6	7	9	8	4	2	1	5	3
1	3	5	4	8	9	6	7	2
2	6	8	7	1	5	9	3	4
4	9	7	2	6	3	5	8	1
7	5	4	9	2	8	3	1	6
9	8	6	3	7	1	4	2	5
3	1	2	6	5	4	7	9	8

Puzzle # 2

2	9	7	4	1	5	8	3	6
6	3	5	7	9	8	1	4	2
4	1	8	2	3	6	7	9	5
8	2	9	6	7	3	5	1	4
7	5	3	8	4	1	2	6	9
1	6	4	9	5	2	3	7	8
9	8	6	3	2	7	4	5	1
3	4	1	5	8	9	6	2	7
5	7	2	1	6	4	9	8	3

Puzzle # 3

5	7	6	2	1	4	9	3	8
1	9	8	3	6	5	4	7	2
4	3	2	9	8	7	5	6	1
9	2	4	7	5	1	6	8	3
7	5	3	8	9	6	1	2	4
6	8	1	4	3	2	7	5	9
3	6	5	1	2	9	8	4	7
2	4	9	6	7	8	3	1	5
8	1	7	5	4	3	2	9	6

Puzzle # 4

9	3	2	6	4	5	7	1	8
6	5	8	7	1	2	9	4	3
7	1	4	9	8	3	2	5	6
5	6	9	1	2	4	3	8	7
3	4	1	8	7	9	6	2	5
2	8	7	3	5	6	4	9	1
8	9	6	4	3	1	5	7	2
1	2	3	5	9	7	8	6	4
4	7	5	2	6	8	1	3	9

Puzzle # 5

8	5	9	2	4	6	3	7	1
2	4	7	1	3	9	6	8	5
6	1	3	5	8	7	9	4	2
3	2	1	4	7	5	8	9	6
9	6	4	3	2	8	5	1	7
5	7	8	6	9	1	4	2	3
4	9	5	7	6	2	1	3	8
7	3	6	8	1	4	2	5	9
1	8	2	9	5	3	7	6	4

Puzzle # 6

2	1	8	4	5	6	9	3	7
5	3	4	2	7	9	8	1	6
7	9	6	3	8	1	4	5	2
8	6	3	7	1	5	2	9	4
4	5	2	8	9	3	6	7	1
9	7	1	6	4	2	5	8	3
3	8	9	1	2	4	7	6	5
6	2	5	9	3	7	1	4	8
1	4	7	5	6	8	3	2	9

Puzzle # 7

7	6	3	8	4	1	9	2	5
1	8	9	3	5	2	4	6	7
4	5	2	6	7	9	1	8	3
6	2	7	4	9	5	3	1	8
3	4	8	2	1	6	5	7	9
9	1	5	7	8	3	6	4	2
2	7	6	9	3	4	8	5	1
5	3	4	1	2	8	7	9	6
8	9	1	5	6	7	2	3	4

Puzzle # 8

8	2	1	5	9	3	6	7	4
3	4	5	2	7	6	1	9	8
7	9	6	4	8	1	3	5	2
6	5	9	3	2	8	7	4	1
2	8	4	7	1	5	9	6	3
1	7	3	9	6	4	2	8	5
9	3	8	1	5	7	4	2	6
4	6	2	8	3	9	5	1	7
5	1	7	6	4	2	8	3	9

Puzzle # 9

9	5	3	8	7	2	4	6	1
7	6	4	3	5	1	2	9	8
2	8	1	4	9	6	7	5	3
6	4	5	2	1	9	8	3	7
3	2	9	7	8	5	1	4	6
1	7	8	6	3	4	9	2	5
5	3	2	1	4	8	6	7	9
4	1	7	9	6	3	5	8	2
8	9	6	5	2	7	3	1	4

Puzzle # 10

4	8	3	1	7	9	5	6	2
9	2	1	4	5	6	8	3	7
5	7	6	8	2	3	1	9	4
6	4	5	2	9	1	7	8	3
2	1	7	3	4	8	6	5	9
8	3	9	7	6	5	4	2	1
7	5	8	9	1	2	3	4	6
1	6	2	5	3	4	9	7	8
3	9	4	6	8	7	2	1	5

Puzzle # 11

6	2	8	9	5	7	3	4	1
3	4	9	6	1	2	8	7	5
5	1	7	4	3	8	6	2	9
9	6	4	2	7	1	5	8	3
2	3	1	5	8	4	9	6	7
8	7	5	3	6	9	2	1	4
7	9	3	1	2	6	4	5	8
4	8	2	7	9	5	1	3	6
1	5	6	8	4	3	7	9	2

Puzzle # 12

9	6	2	7	8	5	4	3	1
5	1	8	3	4	2	7	9	6
3	7	4	1	9	6	8	2	5
8	2	3	4	7	1	6	5	9
1	9	6	5	2	8	3	7	4
7	4	5	9	6	3	1	8	2
6	8	1	2	3	9	5	4	7
4	3	9	6	5	7	2	1	8
2	5	7	8	1	4	9	6	3

Puzzle # 13

5	4	9	7	2	6	3	1	8
6	8	3	1	5	9	7	4	2
7	2	1	4	8	3	6	9	5
3	6	4	9	1	5	8	2	7
2	7	5	6	4	8	9	3	1
1	9	8	3	7	2	4	5	6
4	5	6	8	9	1	2	7	3
9	3	2	5	6	7	1	8	4
8	1	7	2	3	4	5	6	9

Puzzle # 14

7	1	5	4	9	8	6	3	2
9	6	2	5	7	3	4	1	8
4	8	3	6	2	1	7	5	9
1	2	8	9	6	4	5	7	3
5	9	4	3	8	7	2	6	1
6	3	7	1	5	2	9	8	4
2	5	1	7	3	9	8	4	6
8	4	6	2	1	5	3	9	7
3	7	9	8	4	6	1	2	5

Puzzle # 15

6	3	7	4	9	2	5	1	8
9	2	5	7	8	1	6	3	4
1	8	4	3	6	5	9	2	7
3	4	6	8	2	7	1	5	9
8	9	2	5	1	4	7	6	3
7	5	1	6	3	9	8	4	2
2	7	9	1	4	6	3	8	5
5	1	8	2	7	3	4	9	6
4	6	3	9	5	8	2	7	1

Puzzle # 16

6	5	1	4	9	2	8	7	3
4	9	2	8	7	3	1	6	5
3	7	8	6	5	1	4	2	9
1	4	3	9	6	8	2	5	7
2	6	7	3	1	5	9	4	8
5	8	9	2	4	7	6	3	1
9	3	6	7	8	4	5	1	2
8	2	5	1	3	6	7	9	4
7	1	4	5	2	9	3	8	6

Puzzle # 17

8	4	1	6	9	2	7	3	5
7	3	2	4	5	1	8	6	9
6	9	5	7	3	8	1	4	2
2	1	7	9	8	4	6	5	3
4	6	9	5	1	3	2	8	7
3	5	8	2	7	6	4	9	1
1	7	4	3	6	9	5	2	8
9	8	6	1	2	5	3	7	4
5	2	3	8	4	7	9	1	6

Puzzle # 18

5	8	6	1	3	4	2	9	7
7	1	4	9	5	2	6	8	3
3	9	2	6	7	8	1	4	5
2	6	3	4	9	7	8	5	1
1	5	8	3	2	6	4	7	9
9	4	7	5	8	1	3	6	2
6	3	1	7	4	9	5	2	8
8	7	5	2	6	3	9	1	4
4	2	9	8	1	5	7	3	6

Puzzle # 19

7	8	3	2	5	9	6	1	4
6	2	4	3	8	1	9	7	5
1	5	9	7	4	6	2	8	3
5	3	7	9	6	4	1	2	8
9	4	8	1	2	7	5	3	6
2	1	6	5	3	8	4	9	7
8	9	1	6	7	5	3	4	2
4	6	2	8	9	3	7	5	1
3	7	5	4	1	2	8	6	9

Puzzle # 20

1	6	4	2	7	9	8	3	5
2	3	7	5	8	4	1	6	9
9	8	5	6	3	1	2	7	4
4	2	1	9	5	3	7	8	6
5	7	3	8	6	2	4	9	1
6	9	8	1	4	7	3	5	2
8	5	2	7	1	6	9	4	3
7	4	9	3	2	5	6	1	8
3	1	6	4	9	8	5	2	7

Puzzle # 21

6	8	9	7	2	4	3	5	1
3	7	2	1	8	5	9	6	4
5	1	4	3	6	9	2	8	7
4	9	5	2	7	8	6	1	3
8	2	1	4	3	6	7	9	5
7	3	6	9	5	1	4	2	8
1	5	3	6	4	2	8	7	9
9	6	7	8	1	3	5	4	2
2	4	8	5	9	7	1	3	6

Puzzle # 22

5	4	1	8	3	6	9	7	2
7	9	6	4	1	2	8	5	3
3	8	2	5	7	9	1	4	6
2	5	7	1	9	3	4	6	8
4	1	9	7	6	8	3	2	5
6	3	8	2	4	5	7	9	1
1	2	5	9	8	4	6	3	7
8	6	4	3	2	7	5	1	9
9	7	3	6	5	1	2	8	4

Puzzle # 23

5	9	8	3	7	4	2	1	6
7	2	4	8	1	6	5	9	3
3	1	6	2	9	5	4	7	8
2	6	5	1	4	3	9	8	7
4	8	3	7	6	9	1	5	2
1	7	9	5	8	2	3	6	4
8	3	7	4	5	1	6	2	9
9	5	2	6	3	7	8	4	1
6	4	1	9	2	8	7	3	5

Puzzle # 24

3	2	7	9	4	8	1	6	5
8	6	5	2	3	1	7	9	4
4	9	1	6	7	5	3	8	2
9	5	3	7	1	2	6	4	8
2	1	6	8	9	4	5	7	3
7	8	4	5	6	3	2	1	9
6	4	2	3	8	7	9	5	1
5	7	8	1	2	9	4	3	6
1	3	9	4	5	6	8	2	7

Word Searches

Puzzle #1

MILK

B	L	R	U	F	C	L	A	E	R	E	C	G	D	X
R	M	L	E	Y	A	E	E	M	S	Y	O	O	R	U
E	M	B	U	T	R	R	E	M	F	E	V	A	W	Q
A	T	G	W	B	T	I	M	F	U	I	E	T	U	O
K	S	K	I	M	O	U	A	W	F	S	P	H	B	H
F	D	S	R	C	N	B	B	D	P	O	C	H	C	O
A	E	T	A	L	O	C	O	H	C	C	C	L	I	P
S	C	O	O	K	I	E	S	C	R	E	A	M	E	R
T	T	P	Z	Z	D	C	M	I	L	K	M	A	N	S
N	I	E	T	O	R	P	E	S	R	E	D	D	U	D
A	U	N	O	I	T	A	T	C	A	L	B	A	Y	A
M	I	L	K	S	H	A	K	E	R	N	C	I	J	N
S	T	R	A	W	B	E	R	R	Y	E	D	H	F	Q
M	Z	A	Z	Q	M	F	I	A	W	V	A	T	Q	R
Q	V	W	V	G	B	Z	H	X	X	O	Z	M	R	Z

BREAKFAST
BULL
BUTTER
CARTON
CEREAL
CHEESE
CHOCOLATE
COFFEE
COOKIES
COW
CREAMER
DAIRY
FARM
GOAT
ICE CREAM
LACTATION
MILKMAN
MILKSHAKE
MUSCLES
PROTEIN
SKIM
STRAWBERRY
UDDERS

Puzzle #2

JOBS

A	R	A	B	B	T	B	F	E	H	C	C	E	E	C
R	C	O	T	A	A	S	U	R	S	D	F	Y	D	U
T	C	C	T	H	K	N	I	T	O	R	E	A	I	S
I	Q	A	O	C	L	E	K	G	C	T	U	K	T	T
S	U	D	R	U	A	E	R	E	O	H	C	N	O	O
T	A	E	M	P	N	E	T	E	R	L	E	O	R	D
M	R	E	D	L	E	T	V	E	E	E	O	R	D	I
R	E	M	R	A	F	N	A	I	T	N	Y	I	J	A
T	S	I	T	N	E	D	T	N	T	W	I	W	B	N
R	E	N	E	D	R	A	G	E	T	C	G	G	A	W
N	A	M	R	E	H	S	I	F	R	M	E	H	N	L
N	A	I	C	I	R	T	C	E	L	E	M	T	U	E
F	I	R	E	F	I	G	H	T	E	R	R	W	E	E
H	A	I	R	D	R	E	S	S	E	R	L	C	U	D
R	E	P	A	C	S	D	N	A	L	H	L	C	Y	E

ACCOUNTANT
ACTOR
ARTIST
ATHLETE
BAKER
BANKER
BIOLOGIST
BUTCHER
CARPENTER
CHEF
CUSTODIAN
DENTIST
DETECTIVE
DOCTOR
EDITOR
ELECTRICIAN
ENGINEER
FARMER
FIREFIGHTER
FISHERMAN
GARDENER
HAIRDRESSER
LANDSCAPER
LAWYER

Puzzle #3

MUSICAL INSTRUMENTS

F	R	E	N	C	H	H	O	R	N	O	J	N	A	B
C	E	L	L	O	B	A	G	P	I	P	E	F	H	S
F	L	U	T	E	I	N	O	O	S	S	A	B	A	A
R	A	A	M	U	R	D	H	A	R	P	S	O	R	X
M	A	C	R	A	T	A	R	E	O	B	O	E	P	O
T	U	T	I	I	N	R	B	O	N	A	I	P	S	P
R	U	R	I	N	N	D	U	U	C	J	T	T	I	H
O	N	K	D	U	O	E	O	M	T	C	X	C	C	O
M	M	Y	U	L	G	M	T	L	P	C	A	D	H	N
B	G	C	Q	L	E	K	R	I	I	E	B	L	O	E
O	X	V	E	S	E	E	O	A	L	N	T	F	R	L
N	V	I	O	L	A	L	T	S	H	Q	C	W	D	M
E	N	I	L	O	I	V	E	S	A	W	H	A	G	F
T	A	M	B	O	U	R	I	N	E	X	I	A	P	E
X	Y	L	O	P	H	O	N	E	F	D	J	M	I	X

ACCORDION
BAGPIPE
BANJO
BASSOON
CELLO
CLARINET
DRUM
FLUTE
FRENCH HORN
GUITAR
HARMONICA
HARP
HARPSICHORD
MANDOLIN
OBOE
PIANO
SAXOPHONE
STEEL DRUM
TAMBOURINE
TROMBONE
TRUMPET
TUBA
UKULELE
VIOLA
VIOLIN
XYLOPHONE

Puzzle #4

MONEY

B	K	Y	L	L	I	B	U	D	G	E	T	X	I	G
H	A	N	C	Y	D	E	B	T	E	A	C	N	A	L
V	S	L	A	T	C	I	I	P	M	P	Z	O	E	T
Z	K	A	A	B	P	N	M	N	E	U	O	U	V	C
T	K	G	C	N	S	U	E	E	C	N	K	S	F	D
R	I	C	H	Q	C	C	R	R	W	O	N	Q	I	U
D	O	L	L	A	R	E	I	K	R	L	M	Y	N	T
S	G	N	I	N	R	A	E	M	N	U	W	E	A	P
Q	N	I	T	S	P	V	U	J	O	A	C	Z	N	A
U	G	C	L	I	A	P	R	O	U	N	B	T	C	Y
A	G	K	E	W	F	V	P	N	U	Z	O	L	E	M
R	X	E	I	F	S	O	I	D	T	I	C	C	M	E
T	V	L	X	Q	K	J	R	N	G	C	M	I	E	N
E	W	D	D	C	Y	U	T	P	G	L	R	E	Z	T
R	N	O	I	S	S	E	C	E	R	S	V	V	S	M

BALANCE	DEBT	NICKEL
BANK	DEPOSIT	PAYMENT
BANKRUPTCY	DIME	PENNY
BILL	DOLLAR	PROFIT
BUDGET	EARNINGS	QUARTER
CASH	ECONOMICS	RECESSION
CENT	FINANCE	RICH
CURRENCY	INCOME	SAVINGS

Puzzle #5

TOOLS

H	C	N	E	R	W	N	E	L	L	A	Y	D	V	R
R	F	F	G	X	S	R	E	P	I	L	A	C	I	A
C	L	A	M	P	A	L	E	S	I	H	C	A	S	A
C	R	O	W	B	A	R	D	G	H	A	M	M	E	R
H	L	M	P	A	P	R	E	R	R	E	D	D	A	L
L	A	E	A	L	S	L	E	T	I	I	T	V	C	R
F	E	C	V	L	A	G	I	L	U	L	N	V	V	D
V	S	V	K	E	L	N	I	E	U	O	L	D	K	C
S	K	X	O	S	L	E	E	J	R	R	R	V	E	M
X	M	C	Y	H	A	F	T	H	F	S	G	U	K	R
X	T	T	T	G	S	W	E	X	A	K	C	I	P	A
R	E	V	I	R	D	W	E	R	C	S	X	I	B	R
X	O	B	L	O	O	T	R	O	W	E	L	N	T	Q
W	R	E	N	C	H	Y	L	K	H	A	L	I	H	W
L	K	T	U	V	S	L	R	S	L	A	X	M	C	O

ALLEN WRENCH
AXE
CALIPERS
CHISEL
CLAMP
CROWBAR
DRILL
GRINDER
HACKSAW
HAMMER
JIGSAW
LADDER
LEVEL
MALLET
PICKAXE
PLANE
PLIERS
ROUTER
RULER
SCREWDRIVER
SHOVEL
TOOLBOX
TROWEL
VISE
WRENCH

Puzzle #6

SCIENCE

Y	R	A	L	D	B	Y	G	O	L	O	I	B	K	T
U	M	T	H	A	A	L	E	G	E	O	L	O	G	Y
K	F	O	T	T	C	T	L	T	M	P	L	T	B	G
Y	M	M	N	N	T	I	A	E	A	S	S	A	M	R
E	G	G	X	O	E	M	M	T	C	M	E	N	D	A
H	V	R	J	Q	R	M	A	E	C	H	I	Y	Z	V
Y	J	O	E	J	I	T	E	U	H	X	R	L	E	I
P	V	G	L	N	A	M	S	L	F	C	E	T	C	T
O	O	E	J	U	E	L	Z	A	E	X	S	E	J	Y
T	J	I	Q	J	T	N	E	M	I	R	E	P	X	E
H	D	W	V	J	A	I	R	E	T	T	A	M	W	S
E	Y	R	O	T	A	R	O	B	A	L	R	T	J	G
S	C	I	S	Y	H	P	V	N	A	F	C	K	G	Q
I	M	I	C	R	O	S	C	O	P	E	H	R	A	Q
S	M	O	L	E	C	U	L	E	H	Q	S	V	Z	Z

ASTRONOMY
ATOM
BACTERIA
BIOLOGY
BOTANY
CELL
CHEMICAL
CLIMATE
DATA
ELEMENT
ENERGY
EVOLUTION
EXPERIMENT
GEOLOGY
GRAVITY
HYPOTHESIS
LABORATORY
MASS
MATTER
MICROSCOPE
MOLECULE
PHYSICS
RESEARCH

Puzzle #7

RESTAURANT

R	E	Z	I	T	E	P	P	A	B	B	F	T	W	N
D	Q	G	J	D	H	C	F	X	E	I	U	E	T	J
Y	E	K	A	D	A	C	H	H	E	L	H	N	H	A
H	O	L	C	R	Z	E	N	I	F	L	R	Y	E	C
B	R	A	I	S	E	D	R	U	C	W	V	R	Q	M
E	S	R	U	O	C	V	L	B	R	K	Q	R	W	T
B	O	H	E	M	B	X	E	H	Z	B	E	W	D	Y
T	S	A	F	K	A	E	R	B	G	N	I	N	I	D
C	O	N	D	I	M	E	N	T	S	Y	R	T	H	M
N	E	S	S	E	T	A	C	I	L	E	D	P	C	S
G	A	B	E	I	G	G	O	D	E	N	T	R	E	E
T	E	M	R	U	O	G	H	O	S	T	E	S	S	R
E	S	R	U	O	C	N	I	A	M	O	I	X	E	V
N	A	P	K	I	N	N	F	N	E	L	O	J	C	E
N	O	I	T	A	V	R	E	S	E	R	K	B	N	R

APPETIZER
BEEF
BEVERAGE
BILL
BOILED
BRAISED
BREAD
BREAKFAST

BRUNCH
CHEF
CHICKEN
CONDIMENTS
COURSE
DELICATESSEN
DINING
DOGGIE BAG

ENTREE
GOURMET
HOSTESS
MAIN COURSE
MENU
NAPKIN
RESERVATION
SERVER

Puzzle #8

US STATES

A	A	R	K	A	N	S	A	S	N	A	K	C	M	P
L	K	N	O	I	I	M	O	W	U	V	X	O	I	X
A	H	S	O	H	N	N	A	I	O	T	V	L	S	C
B	P	A	A	Z	A	D	R	I	H	I	L	O	S	K
A	X	U	T	L	I	D	I	O	N	O	N	R	O	T
M	D	C	F	U	A	R	I	A	F	E	U	A	U	F
A	G	E	O	R	G	I	A	M	N	I	L	D	R	Q
Y	L	O	U	I	S	I	A	N	A	A	L	O	I	E
I	K	D	N	A	L	Y	R	A	M	B	X	A	R	V
T	V	C	N	A	G	I	H	C	I	M	M	D	C	F
I	P	N	U	A	T	O	S	E	N	N	I	M	N	A
F	M	O	N	T	A	N	A	K	S	A	R	B	E	N
O	R	E	G	O	N	E	V	A	D	A	A	Z	K	Y
T	E	X	A	S	T	E	O	K	L	A	H	O	M	A
A	M	J	H	C	K	G	K	B	Y	H	F	J	I	I

ALABAMA
ALASKA
ARIZONA
ARKANSAS
CALIFORNIA
COLORADO
GEORGIA
IDAHO
INDIANA
IOWA
KANSAS
KENTUCKY
LOUISIANA
MAINE
MARYLAND
MICHIGAN
MINNESOTA
MISSOURI
MONTANA
NEBRASKA
NEVADA
OHIO
OKLAHOMA
OREGON
TEXAS
UTAH

Word Searches

answers

MILK
Puzzle # 1

B	L	R		F	C	L	A	E	R	E	C	G		
R		L	E	Y	A	E			S			O		
E			U	T	R	R	E	M		E		A	W	
A				B	T	I	M	F	U		E	T		
K	S	K	I	M	O	U	A		F	S		H		
F					N		B	D		O	C		C	
A	E	T	A	L	O	C	O	H	C		C	L		
S	C	O	O	K	I	E	S	C	R	E	A	M	E	R
T						C	M	I	L	K	M	A	N	S
N	I	E	T	O	R	P	E	S	R	E	D	D	U	
		N	O	I	T	A	T	C	A	L				
M	I	L	K	S	H	A	K	E	R					
S	T	R	A	W	B	E	R	R	Y	E				
											A			
												M		

JOBS
Puzzle # 2

A	R	A	B	B	T	B	F	E	H	C			E	C
R	C	O	T	A	A	S	U	R	S				D	U
T	C	C	T	H	K	N	I	T	O	R			I	S
I		A	O	C	L	E	K	G	C	T	U		T	T
S			R	U	A	E	R	E	O	H	C	N	O	O
T				P	N	E	T	E	R	L	E	O	R	D
					E	T	V	E	E	E	O	R	D	I
R	E	M	R	A	F	N	A	I		N	Y	I		A
T	S	I	T	N	E	D	T	N	T		I	W	B	N
R	E	N	E	D	R	A	G	E	T	C		G	A	
N	A	M	R	E	H	S	I	F	R		E		N	L
N	A	I	C	I	R	T	C	E	L	E		T		E
F	I	R	E	F	I	G	H	T	E	R			E	
H	A	I	R	D	R	E	S	S	E	R				D
R	E	P	A	C	S	D	N	A	L					

MUSICAL INSTRUMENTS
Puzzle # 3

F	R	E	N	C	H	H	O	R	N	O	J	N	A	B
C	E	L	L	O	B	A	G	P	I	P	E		H	S
F	L	U	T	E	I	N	O	O	S	S	A	B	A	A
R	A	A	M	U	R	D	H	A	R	P			R	X
M	A	C	R	A	T	A	R	E	O	B	O		P	O
T	U	T	I	I	N	R	B	O	N	A	I	P	S	P
R	U	R	I	N	N	D	U	U	C				I	H
O		K	D	U	O	E	O	M	T	C			C	O
M			U	L	G	M	T	L	P		A		H	N
B				L	E		R		I	E			O	E
O					E	E		A		N	T		R	
N	V	I	O	L	A	L	T		H				D	
E	N	I	L	O	I	V	E	S						
T	A	M	B	O	U	R	I	N	E					
X	Y	L	O	P	H	O	N	E						

MONEY
Puzzle # 4

B	K	Y	L	L	I	B	U	D	G	E	T	X		
H	A	N	C	Y	D	E	B	T	E			N	A	
	S	L	A	T	C	I	I	P		P			E	T
		A	A	B	P	N	M	N	E		O			C
			C	N	S	U	E	E	C	N		S	F	
R	I	C	H		C	C	R	R		O	N		I	
D	O	L	L	A	R	E	I	K	R		M	Y	N	T
S	G	N	I	N	R	A	E	M	N	U		E	A	P
Q		I	T	S					O	A	C		N	A
U		C		I	A					N	B		C	Y
A		K			F	V					O		E	M
R		E				O	I					C		E
T		L					R	N					E	N
E								P	G					T
R	N	O	I	S	S	E	C	E	R	S				

TOOLS
Puzzle # 5

H	C	N	E	R	W	N	E	L	L	A			V	
				X	S	R	E	P	I	L	A	C	I	
C	L	A	M	P	A	L	E	S	I	H	C		S	
C	R	O	W	B	A	R	D	G	H	A	M	M	E	R
H	L	M	P	A	P	R	E	R	R	E	D	D	A	L
L	A	E	A	L	S	L	E	T	I	I				
	E	C	V	L	A	G	I	L	U	L	N			
		V	K	E	L	N	I	E	U	O	L	D		
			O	S	L	E	E	J	R	R	R		E	
				H	A		T			S				R
					S	W	E	X	A	K	C	I	P	
R	E	V	I	R	D	W	E	R	C	S				
X	O	B	L	O	O	T	R	O	W	E	L			
W	R	E	N	C	H									

SCIENCE
Puzzle # 6

Y		A	L	D	B	Y	G	O	L	O	I	B		
	M	T		A	A	L	E	G	E	O	L	O	G	Y
		O	T		C	T	L	T				T		G
Y		M	N	N	T	I	A	E	A	S	S	A	M	R
E	G			O	E		M		C	M		N		A
H	V	R			R	M		E			I	Y		V
Y		O	E		I	T	E		H		R	L		I
P			L	N	A		S	L		C	E		C	T
O				U	E			A	E		S			Y
T					T	N	E	M	I	R	E	P	X	E
H						I	R	E	T	T	A	M		
E	Y	R	O	T	A	R	O	B	A	L	R			
S	C	I	S	Y	H	P		N			C			
I	M	I	C	R	O	S	C	O	P	E	H			
S	M	O	L	E	C	U	L	E						

RESTAURANT
Puzzle # 7

R	E	Z	I	T	E	P	P	A	B	B	F			
D		G		D	H	C			E	I	U	E		
	E		A		A	C	H		E	L		N	H	
		L		R		E	N	I	F	L			E	C
B	R	A	I	S	E	D	R	U	C					M
E	S	R	U	O	C	V		B	R	K				
					B		E			B	E			
T	S	A	F	K	A	E	R	B	G	N	I	N	I	D
C	O	N	D	I	M	E	N	T	S					
N	E	S	S	E	T	A	C	I	L	E	D			S
G	A	B	E	I	G	G	O	D	E	N	T	R	E	E
T	E	M	R	U	O	G	H	O	S	T	E	S	S	R
E	S	R	U	O	C	N	I	A	M					V
N	A	P	K	I	N									E
N	O	I	T	A	V	R	E	S	E	R				R

US STATES
Puzzle # 8

A	A	R	K	A	N	S	A	S	N	A	K	C	M	
L	K	N	O	I	I	M	O	W				O	I	
A	H	S	O	H	N	N	A	I	O			L	S	
B		A	A	Z	A	D	R	I	H	I		O	S	
A			T	L	I	D	I	O	N	O		R	O	
M				U	A	R	I	A	F	E		A	U	
A	G	E	O	R	G	I	A		N	I		D	R	
Y	L	O	U	I	S	I	A	N	A	A	L	O	I	
	K	D	N	A	L	Y	R	A	M			A		
		C	N	A	G	I	H	C	I	M			C	
			U	A	T	O	S	E	N	N	I	M		
	M	O	N	T	A	N	A	K	S	A	R	B	E	N
O	R	E	G	O	N	E	V	A	D	A				
T	E	X	A	S		E	O	K	L	A	H	O	M	A
							K							

End

www.ingramcontent.com/pod-product-compliance
Lightning Source LLC
Chambersburg PA
CBHW080609220526
45466CB00010B/3298

* 9 7 9 8 5 6 7 5 9 2 9 9 1 *